George Mathews

Joseph Benson Foraker

Sketch of the Cincinnati Banquet given in his Honor on the Occasion of his

Election as Senator of the United States for Ohio, February 22, 1896

George Mathews

Joseph Benson Foraker
Sketch of the Cincinnati Banquet given in his Honor on the Occasion of his Election as Senator of the United States for Ohio, February 22, 1896

ISBN/EAN: 9783337154158

Printed in Europe, USA, Canada, Australia, Japan

Cover: Foto ©ninafisch / pixelio.de

More available books at **www.hansebooks.com**

» Testimonial Souvenir «

Joseph Benson Foraker

Sketch of the Cincinnati Banquet given in his Honor on the Occasion of his
Election as Senator of the United States for Ohio,
February 22, 1896

❧

" A Patriot's is a dangerous post
When wanted by his Country most "
— *Scott.*

Under Direction of Senator Foraker's Friends

By George Mathews

Cincinnati, 1896

A TRIBUTE.

In leadership the foremost man is he
    Who stands for country and, with lifted hand
    Calls to the patriot people! his command—
A clarion cry heard far by land and sea—
Awakes the holy passions of the free!
    Grave senates hear him, and his native land
    Makes him her watchman in her towers, to stand
And cry the "All is well" of Liberty!

Lo, such is he who rises for his State,
    And leads her thought, and battles in her cause,
        And wears fresh laurels in her glorious name!
Hero and captain, champion in debate,
    Man of the people, maker of their laws,
        Neighbor, and friend, and statesman full of fame.

Joseph Benson Foraker.

Prefatory

THE occasion which has called forth this simple brochure and tribute is easily understood. A distinguished citizen of Ohio, honored by the people of the Commonwealth, received on the birthday of the Father of our Country, 1896, a testimonial banquet given by the citizens of Cincinnati as a mark of their esteem and admiration. The recipient of this honor was Senator-elect Joseph Benson Foraker, whose name for a full score of years has been identified with the public life of Ohio. The recent mark of esteem and confidence was one of many such tributes, but it had an important and peculiar significance. The event distinguished the accession of Mr. Foraker to one of the highest electoral dignities in the gift of any people.

The United States is the greatest free government in the world. The Senate of the United States has no equal as a body of deliberative councilors. It is peculiarly constituted. Its members represent commonwealths as such, and the peoples of the respective commonwealths in their aggregate and several capacities. Though all Senators are of equal rank, there is a sense in which they are most unequal. In their representative capacity they may stand for small commonwealths, or for states of imperial extent.

Such an imperial State is Ohio. Third among the members of the Union in population and wealth, she may be regarded as one of the greatest free communities existing on earth. To represent such a State in the greatest senatorial body of the world, is a distinction of which the most ambitious citizen may well be proud. To be called to such a station at a time of life when most men are still regarded as young, correspondingly increases the honor. It is proper that a recipient of so great a distinction should feel a manly and ennobling sentiment of pride at the honor done him by his fellow-countrymen.

Joseph B. Foraker is a man so honored. He is Senator-elect from the great state of Ohio. He is a Cincinnatian. He has long been identified with the public welfare of this great city, and the people of Cincinnati have recognized in this event an opportunity of compliment to a leading citizen.

It has been thought that the complimentary banquet given to Mr. Foraker at the Cathedral of the Scottish Rite in token of the appreciation of the people of Cincinnati, should not pass without leaving some record of itself more permanent than the passing memory of a busy population. It is for this reason that the facts, circumstances and speeches of the occasion have been gathered and put into a permanent form in this testimonial pamphlet which is sent to the friends of Senator Foraker as a token of friendship and goodwill.

The Senator is not himself responsible for this publication, or for the terms of compliment in which it is made. It is wholly the work of his friends, who design it as a tribute to a man who has won the applause of the Nation, and at the same time retained the affectionate regard and confidence of his friends and neighbors.

Biographical.

JOSEPH BENSON FORAKER, recently elected Junior Senator of the United States from Ohio, is a native of this Commonwealth. He was born near Rainsborough in Highland County, Ohio, on the 5th of July, 1846. He has not yet completed his fiftieth year. In both mind and body he is young, elastic, full of spirits, warmed with a laudable ambition, and kindled with what the author of *Ecce Homo* calls "enthusiasm of humanity." The parents of Senator Foraker are still living. They belong to the class of people who cultivate the soil, and at the same time cultivate men and women. Joseph B. Foraker spent the first years of his life on a farm in close touch with the ground and in sympathy with the ennobling influences of nature.

Passing from the period of his early boyhood, and with no note of his school-days in the country, we find him at the *age of sixteen* enlisting in the Union Army. He volunteered as a member of Company A, in the 89th Regiment of Ohio Volunteers. The date of his enlistment was July 14, 1862, nine days after his sixteenth anniversary. A young soldier — but many such followed the flag and fought our battle.

Young Foraker served with his regiment until after the fall of Atlanta. By that date he had risen to the rank of First Lieutenant. After the capture of Atlanta he was detailed for service in the signal corps and was assigned to duty as a signal officer on the staff of Major-General Slocum, who was in command at that time of the left wing of Sherman's army.

After the march through Georgia and the Carolinas Lieutenant Foraker was promoted to the rank of Brevet-Captain
of United States Volunteers and was assigned to duty as
Aide-de-camp on the staff of General Slocum. This position he
held until he was mustered out of the service at the close of
the war. That event found him, at the age of nineteen, a
veteran of three years' service.

After the war Captain Foraker resumed the studies which
he had cast aside in order to enlist, and became a student
at Cornell University, Ithaca, N. Y. From that institution he
was graduated at the close of his twenty-third year, in the
summer of 1869. During his collegiate course he took up and
prosecuted the study of law, so that after his graduation he
was able to begin to practice. He came to Cincinnati and was
admitted to the bar on the 14th of October, 1869. From
that date — distant from the present by more than twenty-six
years — he has practiced the duties of his profession in Cincinnati, with only such disturbances as have been incidental to
his public life.

On the 4th of October, 1870, Mr. Foraker was married
to Miss Julia Bundy, daughter of Hon. H. S. Bundy, of
Wellston, Ohio. Of this union have been born five children —
two sons and three daughters — a happy family, all of whom
survive.

The public life of Captain Foraker began in April of 1879,
when he was elected Judge of the Superior Court of Cincinnati. This position he occupied until the first of May, 1882,
when, on account of ill-health, he resigned the duties of the
judgeship. On his recovery, however, he resumed the practice of his profession in the city of his choice. In 1883 he

received the nomination of the Republican Party for Governor of Ohio, but was defeated by his Democratic opponent, Judge Hoadly. In 1884 Mr. Foraker was a delegate to the National Republican Convention and was chairman of the Ohio delegation. In that relation he put in nomination for the Presidency Senator John Sherman. In the following year he was a second time nominated for Governor against Judge Hoadly and was successful. He was chosen Governor of the commonwealth by a handsome majority. In 1887 he was a second time elected to the same office. In the following year he was again a delegate to the Republican National Convention, and was chairman of the delegation from Ohio. In this convention also it was his duty to place John Sherman in nomination for the Presidency, but the nominee failed of gaining a majority of the delegates.

In 1889 Mr. Foraker was for the fourth time named for Governor, but was defeated by ex-Governor James E. Campbell. Mr. Foraker then remained in private life until 1892, when he became a candidate for the office of Senator of the United States for Ohio. He received thirty-eight votes but was defeated by Senator Sherman. In this year he was for the third time delegate at large to the Republican National Convention and served in that body as chairman of the Committee on Resolutions.

By this time the term of Hon. Calvin S. Brice in the United States Senate was drawing to a close and the voice of the people of Ohio was strongly heard in behalf of Mr. Foraker for the position. In the State Convention at Zanesville, held on the 28th of May, 1895, a resolution was unanimously passed endorsing Mr. Foraker as the Republican candidate for United States Senator. At the ensuing November election a Republican legislature was chosen by a majority of over one hundred thousand votes. The sentiment in favor of Mr. Foraker had become overwhelming, and when in January of 1896 the legislature assembled all show of opposition had melted away. Without the formality of a caucus, and by the unanimous vote of his party, he was elected to the Senate of the United States for the term of six years, commencing with the 4th of March, 1897.

The State Republican Convention of 1896 was held in Columbus on the 10th and 11th of March. Senator Foraker presided over the convention as its chairman and was by acclamation chosen for *the fourth time* to represent the State of Ohio as one of its delegates at large to the Republican National Convention to be held at St. Louis on the 16th of the following June.

Such is the briefest outline of the career of one of the great men of Ohio. Senator Foraker is in his prime. He is regarded with admiration not only by the people of the State which he honors and that honors him, but also by the people of the whole Nation. He is primarily a man of the people. His sympathies are broad and patriotic. He is strongly on the side of the people and is devoted to American interests in the highest and best sense of that term. His instincts as an old soldier of the Union are blended with the patriotism of the civilian, composing a character as admirable as it is humane. The good wishes of the people of Ohio will follow him to his high place in the Senate with the same confidence and pride with which they have regarded him in all the previous stages of his eminent career.

The Banquet.

Committee of Arrangements.

***

JOHN A. CALDWELL, Chairman.   ANDREW HICKENLOOPER.

SAMUEL W. TROST, Sec'y.   THOMAS P. EGAN.

GEORGE N. STONE, Treas.   RALPH PETERS.

THOMAS MORRISON.   SAMUEL N. FELTON.

J. G. SCHMIDLAPP.   PERIN LANGDON.

MAURICE J. FREIBERG.   C. M. HOLLOWAY.

SCOTTISH RITE CATHEDRAL.

The Banquet.

THE leading citizens of Cincinnati were unwilling that Senator Foraker should remove to Washington to enter upon his duties without tendering to him some public and formal mark of the esteem in which he is held by his home community. It was determined that a public banquet should be tendered him, and for this purpose the Scottish Rite Cathedral on Broadway was selected and the date of Washington's birthday chosen for the occasion.

The banquet was in all respects a brilliant and successful affair. The guests were, for the most part, citizens of Cincinnati and the personal friends and neighbors of the Senator-elect. They were the men with whom he has been associated in the varied and arduous duties of life for many years. They had watched his progress, had sympathized with him in times when the tide seemed to set against his fortunes, and congratulated him when the wave bore him onward to success and honor. Now they met to pay their tribute to him as a representative of the great commonwealth of Ohio in the Senate of the United States.

Mr. Foraker had not for some days been in good health though his spirits were unabated. It had been feared that he would not be able to participate in the pleasures of the banquet, but it is in the nature of such men to rally according to the occasion. Suffice it to say that the Senator did not disappoint his friends but surprised them rather with the brilliancy and spirit of his manner and address. His speech was marked by all the features which have made his oratory so pleasing and effective; his utterances had the old clear ring; his emphatic declarations of Americanism and patriotism touched the right chord and found a harmonious echo in the hearts of all his hearers.

The table at which the guest of honor and others of his immediate friends sat was beautiful in its arrangement and decorations. The hall in every part was tastefully draped and adorned. The floral decorations were especially fine. Above the principal table "Old Glory" was hung out in several forms and looped up with the figure of an eagle. The motto above was "Our Senator" and this sentiment was repeated in several places. In the center of the flag displayed was the portrait of Senator Foraker done to the life. The Committee of Arrangements had placed behind the speaker's chair a hedge of evergreen which furnished a pleasing background to the distinguished group. The whole surrounding was tasteful and inspiring. The Committee had selected the honored Mayor of Cincinnati, John A. Caldwell, as toast-master. The Mayor never appeared to better advantage: his remarks were received with enthusiasm and were regarded as especially appropriate. The guests were seated and the dinner began at half past seven in the evening. The feast proper lasted about two hours when Mayor Caldwell rapped for order. By this time all chill of formality had passed away and the spirits of those assembled had risen to the level of the occasion. There were none present who did not enter heartily into the celebration.

J. A. CALDWELL.

Speech by Hon. J. A. Caldwell.

OUR GUEST, HON. JOHN A. CALDWELL.

"Heroes in history seem to us poetic, because they are there. But if we should tell the simple truth of some of our neighbors, it would sound like poetry."

FELLOW-CINCINNATIANS:

"Your hearts and mine are glad to-night. On either hand is an every-day trusted friend; across and around this board are our neighbors, our business and professional associates, those whose lives are open books to us. We know the story of their beginnings, of their romances, of their aims and ambitions; of their life achievements and triumphs. We know how much of manliness and worth is written there; we know, and are proud and glad to know, that these, our neighbors and friends stand for much that is greatest and best and most progressive in the Cincinnati of to-day.

Merited distinction—honest fame, can come to no one without his associates and friends, compatriots and fellow-citizens, all being the gainer. The Cincinnatian who wins his spurs in life's contest—who gains the world's applause, and receives signal honors from his fellowmen, places amaranthine garlands over every Cincinnati threshold, and makes a mecca of this fair city to which the hero-worshipers of all time will make sacred pilgrimages.

And we, my fellow-citizens, are met to-night to give expression as best we may, to the personal gratification and happiness it brings to us, that he who is our guest of honor and who is also our fellow-Cincinnatian, our neighbor, and personal, intimate friend, the very man we have long hailed as one of the foremost Cincinnatians—our greatest political leader and chieftain, who we know to be worthy of every preferment that an admiring, loving people can bestow, has again been asked to step up higher—and you and I rejoice and are exceeding glad that this preferment has come to him and with an unanimity of party support unprecedented in all the history of first term elections to the National Senate.

Our guest has long been a commanding national figure, filling the public eye—at once the Richelieu and Admiral Crichton of all that pertains to state-craft and politics, sharing honors with Sherman and McKinley as one of Ohio's political triumvirate, a triumvirate as pre-eminent in national affairs of to-day, as was Ohio's galaxy of generals in the War of the Rebellion—Grant, Sherman, and Sheridan, whose undimming fame shines forth resplendent—the most glorious constellation in all the star-studded night of war.

What memories the very name of Foraker conjures; when the brass throat of war thundered forth his country's need—we see the stripling farmer boy take on the full stature of a man and a hero—and march forth to battle valiantly for freedom and for right. Neither hireling nor dastard he—but a volunteer, brave and true, who wrung promotion from the hand of power by dint of valor and personal merit—a mere boy in years, but in all else a man doing a man's deeds.

We see this soldier put off the uniform and don the garb of the civilian, and take up the humdrum life of a student, the better to equip himself for the walks of peace. We see him adopt one of the learned professions and rise in the line of that profession to the bench of the Superior Court of Cincinnati. We see him take on the burdens of a public career—become the idol of every hustings—whose logic and eloquence and personal magnetism convinced and swayed the multitudes ; all the Nation knew when he was in the saddle, when his trenchant tongue—a keen Damascus blade—was making thrust, and parry, and stroke, that found and laid bare every weakness and flaw in the armor of his adversaries.

We see him become the leader of the young, aggressive, enthusiastic element of his party—binding their hearts to his with cords of steel. We see him twice chosen by the suffrages of the people—Governor of his state and become the very pillar of his party's hope. We see him a man of deep personal convictions; fearless in defense of the right as he sees the right; hating cant and sham, with an especial hatred for all pharisaical hypocrites who wear an—I am holier than thou self-adjusted halo.

We know him as a practical man who believes in practical politics; we know him to be a man of ideas and resources—one who never cries aloud in worship of an echo. We know him for what the whole country knows him, an able statesman, a brilliant orator, a profound thinker—but you and I, my hearers, also know him as a friend and neighbor. We know his heart is a human document in which he writes the names of his friends in indelible characters. We know him as a father, and husband and brother, doing his man's part as only a loving, generous, manly, masterful man can do it—and who fully realizes that station and rank and wealth—the plaudits of his fellow men, the external insignia of success verily brings its own reward—but that beyond the utmost purple of that illimitable ambition, there exists a wider horizon of friendship and love.

The great state of Ohio is wont to produce sons to be proud of—and she is prouder of this younger son; she will see to it that his is no entailed estate, that no law of primogeniture cut him off portionless. She has given him a United States Senatorship, and there is no greater, broader field of action and usefulness, of honor and trust; public or private within the possibilities of man, that her admiring, loving, patriotic people would not be happy to bestow upon our guest of honor —Joseph Benson Foraker—Senator-elect from Ohio.

I have the very great honor and pleasure of presenting the Hon. Joseph Benson Foraker, Senator-elect from Ohio.''

RESPONSE, . Hon. Joseph B. Foraker.

Mr. Mayor and Gentlemen:

'' I wish I knew how better than I do to make fitting response to such an introduction and to such a welcome. Words seem to fail me. I can think of nothing other or better to say than simply, I thank you. (Applause.) That I do with all my heart. I thank you, Mr. Mayor, for the kind words you have so beautifully and so eloquently spoken. I do not know what could make them more gratifying unless it would be that, happily, somehow or other, I could be persuaded I merit them. (Applause.) And I thank you, gentlemen, one and all. If I had been allowed to prearrange the circumstances attending my election to the Senate, I could not have ordered them so as to be more gratifying than they have been down to this point. (Cheers and applause.)

It was gratifying, in the first place, to be elected, as it has been said, without any opposition from my own party. It was gratifying, in the second place, to be elected with so little opposition from the other party. (Laughter and cheers.) And it has been gratifying beyond anything I shall undertake to express for me to have been made the recipient, as I have been, at the hands of my Democratic friends, of constant kindnesses, courtesies and marks of personal regard and personal esteem, from the beginning of this contest until this moment. (Great applause.) But nothing has occurred in all these incidents and features to which I have referred so gratifying as this occasion itself. (Applause.) You, gentlemen, are my neighbors and my friends ; you are the men in whose midst I have lived for more than a quarter of a century. My goings out and comings in have all been in your presence. I am better known to you and by you than to or by anybody else.

For me to see gathered here to-night the representatives of all the professions, and of every kind of business that is pursued in our city ; and especially for me to see gathered here in such goodly numbers my Democratic friends, is gratifying beyond anything I can express. (Great applause.) I thank my Republican friends most sincerely, but I do especially, and from the bottom of my heart, thank my Democratic friends. (Cries of "good, good," and applause.) You make it easy for me to feel, as I do, under such circumstances, in going to the Senate, that I go there to represent the State and the whole State and all the people in the State. (Applause and cheers.) Whenever I can consistently do so, it will be a pleasure to me to serve you. I want to be your Senator, as well as the Senator of my Republican friends. (Renewed applause.)

And now, gentlemen, about that service. I have some misgivings about it. I have never had any experience in a legislative body or any kind of a parliamentary assemblage. I do not know how I will get along. (Cries of 'Oh, you're all right; you'll get along.) I forsee some difficulties. I am so constituted by nature that I reach conclusions quickly, and sometimes have not as much patience as I should have with those who do not agree with me. (Laughter and cheers.) I fear, therefore, that in that 'most august assemblage on earth,' as it has been termed, I shall be wearied and less useful than I otherwise would be when those long, tedious debates occur about which we have been reading so much during the last two or three years. (Applause.) But notwithstanding that drawback, I intend to take the place. There are some compensations to offset it.

In the first place, it is a great compensation to follow in the line of succession such distinguished representatives as Cincinnati has had in that body during our day and generation; (Applause and cries of "good! good!") George E. Pugh (applause), Stanley Matthews (applause), and George H. Pendleton (applause). However we may differ as to their respective political views and opinions, we all can agree in ascribing to them, one and all, irreproachable integrity of character and the highest order of intellectuality. (Great applause.)

There is another compensation in the fact that I am to be the colleague of that grand old representative of Republicanism, who has been there, lo, these many years, in the person of John Sherman. (Applause.) But there is something more attractive than all that to me in going to the Senate at this time. That is the character of questions with which we will have to deal. I do not speak in this connection of partisan questions. If the Democratic party should be in power I imagine I would not have much influence in shaping its policy. (Voice: "You would not; that's right.") (Applause.) If the Republican party be in power its policies are already shaped. (Voice: " That's right.) With practically no dissent, all questions of tariff, reciprocity and currency will be settled according to those policies. The questions I refer to are broader than these.

The time has come when there is an emphatic demand for a wise, broad, patriotic, progressive, aggressive American statesmanship. (Tremendous applause and cheers.) I do not like the idea of our being unable to step out at either our front door or back door, on the Atlantic or the Pacific side, without seeing England's flag floating from all the islands that meet our view with her guns pointing wheresoever she will. (Great applause and renewed cheers.) When the Sandwich Islands come knocking at the door with a Republican form of government and the American flag, I say let them in. (Tremendous applause.) When a civilized country turns civilized war into barbarism, as Spain is doing in Cuba, I say, in the name of this Republic and in the name of republican institutions everywhere, as well as in the name of civilization and Christianity, it is our mission to put a stop to it. (Great applause.) And if as a result the stars and stripes should happen to float over that island, it would be no bad acquisition. (Applause.)

I want to see the Monroe doctrine, recently so much talked about, upheld and enforced against all the world. (Applause.) And I shall stand by the administration that stands for America, be that administration Republican or Democratic. (Cheers.)

I want to see our merchant marine restored. There was a time when our merchant marine was the pride of every American. It is to-day but a mortification to us all. We once carried ninety per cent. of our foreign trade in American bottoms, under the American flag. We now carry less than thirteen per cent. We are paying out annually more than $150,000,000 in gold to foreign ships for transportation of freights and passengers. The time has come to remedy that. The way to remedy it is not with subsidies and bounties, but by going back to the first principles practiced by George Washington and the founders of this Republic when they applied the principles of protection to the water as well as to the land. (Applause.)

I want to see the Congress of the United States provide that the fifty per cent. or more of imports that come into our country free of duty shall come in free, provided they come in American bottoms and under the American flag. (Applause.) I want to see it provided that the dutiable goods brought in American ships shall be allowed a rebate on that account. (Applause.)

And when we make these new reciprocity treaties, which we hope to make soon in the future, I want to see incorporated in every one of them a provision that the goods mentioned in the reciprocity treaty shall have the benefits of that provision, provided they are carried in the ships of the reciprocating countries. (Great applause.) When

that shall be done, as done it can and should be, there will no longer be
an elbowing by Great Britain of the American marine off the waters of
the globe. (Applause.)

Shipbuilding will revive, and once again the flag of the United
States will be seen floating in all the channels of trade and commerce.
(Cheers.) And then after that will follow easily and naturally what we
should have had ere this, an American navy able to protect us, let come
what may. (Applause.) When Mr. Cleveland sent to Congress his
Venezuelan message it had more good results than one. One of its good
results was to impress the American people with our defenseless situa-
tion. We should realize that the great wars of the future, if there be
any at all with which we are to be concerned, are far more likely to be
on the water than on the land. We should order accordingly. It is a
patriotic duty to do it.

Then, there is another thing. I do not want to stop to discuss all
these things, but I read in the newspapers this morning just what I
have been looking for for a long time. I read, as you probably did, that
in the city of New York there was yesterday tendered by Europeans,
the capital to build the Nicaragua Canal. Unless the United States of
America build that canal somebody else will build it. (Voices of
"That's so.") The commerce of the world demands it.

People will not any longer be content sailing ships from the Atlantic
to the Pacific Coast, to go ten thousand miles out of the way around
the Horn, through tempestuous seas and inclement seasons. Every
suggestion of patriotism commands us to do that work. (Applause.)
I want to see the United States build it, and own it, and control it
(applause), without any copartnership with anybody, and without any
other nation having any other right with respect to it except only the
right to use it for peaceful purposes, on payment of such tolls as we
may see fit to levy.

I rejoice my fellow-citizens of Cincinnati, that I shall have opportunity to participate in the solution of these great questions. It is but
little I can do, but in my humble way whatever I can contribute will be
most zealously contributed. (Applause.) These are works worthy of
the American people. If we but prosecute them to that success which is
possible, there is in store for us a destiny greater and grander than any
human language can describe." (Tremendous applause and cheers.)

MAYOR CALDWELL:

Ohio has ever been fortunate in selecting her Governors. They have been men who came from the people and were of the people, and she made no exception in the selection of our present Governor in following that rule. He is a Cincinnatian born; was at one time a market boy, selling the products of his farm from a wagon upon our streets, filled the position of coachman, and he filled these positions with the same zeal, earnestness and integrity with which he is now filling the important position of Governor of Ohio. (Cheers and applause.) I now have the pleasure of presenting the Hon. Asa S. Bushnell, the Governor of Ohio. (Long cheers and applause.)

ASA S. BUSHNELL.

Speech by Gov. Asa S. Bushnell.

OHIO, GOV. ASA S. BUSHNELL.

" Glorious in history : rich in statesmanship : famed in presidents."

MR. TOASTMASTER AND FELLOW CITIZENS :

An ex-governor of the state (not the one here present) said to me on an occasion similar to this—a short time ago—'' When you have responded to the toast ' Ohio' fifty times, as I have, you will get tired of it.'' I am not willing to admit this, for I love Ohio too well to ever tire of sounding her praises. I never hear the name but my pulse quickens and a feeling of pride comes over me that I am one of her citizens.

I feel as the boy did at the revival. The minister requested all those who desired to go to heaven to stand up. All arose but one good-sized boy, who remained quietly in his place. Then the minister asked those who wanted to go to the other place to stand up. Not a soul got up. In astonishment he looked at the boy. '' What is the matter with you, boy? Don't you want to go to either place?'' '' No,'' said he, ''Ohio is good enough for me.'' So I say, Ohio is good enough for me.

But a few days ago I visited the old mother of Ohio—the state of Connecticut. To-day Ohio has five times the population of the mother state, which a little more than a hundred years ago sent from her abundant population a colony of forty-eight of her sturdy sons to found a new state west of the Alleghenies. Landing at Marietta, they established the first settlement in the Northwest Territory, from which has since grown five of the grandest commonwealths of the nation.

Ohio! Grand old Commonwealth ! God bless her and her sons and daughters, wherever they may be. None more loyal than they ; their influence is felt wherever a new settlement is to be founded, a new city built, or a conflict for the right to be fought out !

That she is "glorious in history" I have but to refer to her achievements in war and in peace. And, first, allow me to refer to her achievements in war. She did not do much in the Revolution, but it was not her fault. If she had been born earlier she would have taken part in that struggle. While she took an active part in the Indian wars and furnished more troops than any other northern state for the war with Mexico, it was in the War of the Rebellion—the great conflict for the life of the nation—for the honor of the grand old flag—that she most distinguished herself.

Ohio's response to the call of President Lincoln for 75,000 men was immediate. From all parts of the state came proffers of service from tens of thousands, and on the 19th of April—only four days after the call—the First and Second Regiments of Ohio Volunteers had been organized and were on their way to Washington. The Ohio militia, in pay of the state, was pushed into West Virginia, gained the first victories of the war, and drove out the rebel troops. Thus was West Virginia the gift of Ohio. Governor Debison, Ohio's first war governor, had ere this written, "Ohio must lead throughout the war," and she did. Early in 1864, when more troops were imperative, and President Lincoln was fearful another draft upon the people would result in failure, Governor Brough, Ohio's last war governor, called a convention of the governors of Indiana, Illinois, Iowa and Wisconsin, who, with himself representing Ohio, met on April 21, 1864, and notified Mr. Lincoln that they would furnish him 85,000 men for one hundred days, without a dollar of bounty or a single draft. It was a splendid contribution of the loyal West to the cause of the Union. In sixteen days after the call Ohio had supplied 34,000 men—or nearly one-half the number promised—and put them into the field armed and equipped. The arms of Ohio's sons in the field were sustained by the work of Ohio's daughters at home. As Ohio's soldiers were the first to gain victories, so the women of Ohio were the first to organize aid societies. In five days after the fall of Sumter the Soldiers' Aid Society of Northern Ohio was organized, and these noble women eventually distributed food and clothing to the amount of a million dollars. A similar organization was started in the southern part of the state, which was alike successful.

When the war closed more than one-half the able-bodied men of the state had taken up arms for the Union, and Ohio had shown herself to have been the most efficient of all the states, supplying, as she had, the most successful generals and the largest number of able men in the cabinet of the President and in the councils of the nation.

Ohio is to-day in the very heart of the nation, and, being on its great highway over which its commerce and travel flow and where its people must mingle for an interchange and broadening of ideas, she must be national and broad in her policy and character. Her soil is of the richest and there is no one industry which predominates to give her citizens a one-sided development. Agriculture, manufacture, mining and commerce are so equally divided that she may be said to be the most evenly balanced state in the Union, and to this should be added prominence in education.

The large number of colleges—cheap and accessible everywhere—have given multitudes the prime requisite of the higher education which is mental discipline and the use of the instruments of knowledge. In instructors in learning she has produced a host, and to-day in the department of religion she shows an unsurpassed spirit of Christian enterprise and self-sacrifice, leading all the states in the number of missionaries to heathen lands.

The noble history of Ohio, the heroic character of her sons and daughters, signally shown by the eminent leaders she has produced in every department, will remain an imperishable inspiration to the young born upon her soil, to further advance the commonwealth in everything which will inure to her moral and material grandeur.

" Rich in statesmanship !'' Yes ; in the living and in those who have finished their mission and left their works to follow them. Chase, the great financier, an incident in whose life right here at home I can not refrain from relating. Here was the voting place of the great Secretary, and rarely did he miss coming here from Washington to exercise the right of suffrage. On the occasion of an election in 1863— I think it was—under the old regime, when there was always a great crowd around the polls, Mr. Chase came to his precinct to vote. The crowd separated to make clear a passage for Mr. Chase to reach the window to deposit his ticket. A large, brawny fellow, of Irish nationality, stood somewhat in the way, seeing which some one called out,

"Stand back, Mike, you don't vote the Republican ticket." "I know that," said he, "but don't you suppose I want to see the man that makes the greenbacks?" Mr. Chase smiled and touched his hat to the man who had such great respect for him as the author of the greenbacks, if he could not vote for his party.

Stanton, the great War Secretary! Another statesman of whom Ohioans can all be proud. Then Giddings, Wade, Thurman, Pendleton, and a host of others, make up in part the riches of Ohio in statesmanship. Among those who have contributed, and are yet to add luster to her crown of jewels, are Sherman, McKinley and Foraker.

Virginia, the "Mother of Presidents," was famed for the great chief executives she furnished the nation; but Ohio will herafter contest the title of "Mother of Presidents," and claim for herself that distinction, for what presidents of greater fame than Grant, Hayes and Garfield, men who brought great distinction to their state and to the nation in peace and in war? It is worthy of national consideration that no candidate for president from Ohio was ever defeated.

Ours is a great state in its resources and extent, but greater in its people. I love my state and my country, and I pray to Almighty God that He will give us vigor and energy and power until the pillars of the Union shall be planted so firmly in American soil that no power on earth shall be able to shake them. To make our government thus strong we must stand by it—not complain of it, but praise it; not defame and abuse its highest officials, as has recently been done. While I believe in free speech, I hope that no man will be allowed to use such language in reference to the chief executive of this nation as was uttered in that most august legislative body, the U. S. Senate, by Senator Tillman, of South Carolina, without rebuke. If the statements were true, they were better unsaid; if he had no respect for the chief executive, he should have respect for the high office he holds, for he is the president of the greatest nation on earth. The people of our country should be taught to respect those who have been chosen to make and to execute her laws.

We should adopt such policies as will furnish our government revenue sufficient to meet all obligations and make the nation still richer and still more powerful. To illustrate this, let me relate an incident which came under my observation a few years ago. It

occurred while traveling on the cars in the northern part of the state
with a friend, formerly prominent in the politics of the state, and
known to many of you. My friend, as we rode along, pointed out to
me, first on one side and then the other, beautiful farms, which by
economy and careful investment of his means he had been able to
purchase. Finally, after the last one had been passed and I had
congratulated him on his magnificent possessions, he said, in a half
undertone, and with apparent satisfaction, " Friend Bushnell, a little
money is a good thing to have ; it commands respect at home and
abroad."

Let us have our government rich, that she may build ships of war
and have a navy equal to that of any nation on earth, to the end that
we may demand that more respect be shown our citizens and our flag
on land and sea. We have heard much talk of war of late. Our
nation is not prepared for war ; our navy could not cope with the great
ships of the British. What we want is more money. Let us get that,
then build war vessels, strengthen our forts, and then—though we hope
" war has gone to come again no more "—if it does come, we shall be
prepared for it, and be able to enforce our demand that England shall
be more careful in fixing the boundary lines of her territory.

Ohio must do her part in this further work for the greater glory of
America. Our record has been such that there must be no failure in
the future—no loss of opportunity to prove again that our state is
always ready to advance the cause of Americanism, to do that which
speaks of loyalty to our common flag, and tells again that which has
been a pride to all Ohioans—the patriotism and the strength of our
commonwealth.

I congratulate all—and by that I mean the people of Ohio and
of the nation, as well as those present at this gathering of some of
Cincinnati's foremost citizens—upon the fact that 'another who, by
training, education ability, patriotism and enthusiasm for his country,
will in but a little more than a year's time be received as a member of
America's highest and most distinguished legislative body, and will
therefore add to the fame which has ever attended the Senate of the
United States. We all know this Ohio man. He is the honored
guest of this evening, and one who occupies a more than prominent

place in the affections of the people of this and other states. He is known as a self-made man, as a soldier who achieved a highly honorable record, as a jurist who was respected in all ways, as a chief executive of Ohio who gave a most excellent administration, and as a citizen who enjoys the approval of his fellow-men.

Such a man as Joseph Benson Foraker can be, and I am sure will be, of inestimable value to his country and to his state in the U. S. Senate. He is equipped as few men are for the duty before him, and he has the desire to do his utmost for the common good. I wish him a long life of happiness and continued usefulness ; a life replete with all that can make the hearts of his friends rejoice.

It has given me the greatest pleasure to be present to-night. I have delighted in the opportunity of again attempting to sound a faint measure of praise for my state and our people. It has been a source of sincere gratification to join you in doing honor to my friend Judge Foraker. It has given me great satisfaction again to meet old friends, and to clasp the hands of new ones. Gentlemen of Cincinnati, I congratulate you upon this dinner to your most distinguished citizen, and I thank you for having given me the privilege of addressing you upon so notable an occasion and upon so worthy a topic.

MAYOR CALDWELL :

The next toast, "Our Country." We have with us one of our distinguished citizens, who has gained exceptional prominence in his profession, who will respond to this toast. I have the honor and pleasure of presenting the Hon. E. W. Kittredge. (Long cheers and applause.)

Speech by Hon. E. W. Kittredge.

OUR COUNTRY,   HON. E. W. KITTREDGE.

" Be there a man with soul so dead
Who never to himself hath said,
This is my own, my native land! "

MR. CHAIRMAN AND GENTLEMEN:

The toast "Our Country," to be responded to on Washington's
birthday, naturally recalls Washington's excellently wise advice to his
countrymen as to the relations it should be our policy to maintain with
the nations of Europe.

The position of the United States as the foremost nation on the
American continent is not merely one that should contribute to our
national pride, and still less should it be allowed to stimulate any
national arrogance, but it does carry with it a corresponding duty of
high obligation to all the American nationalities.

The peoples of the old world are organized under powerful governments, with immense resources, with powerful armies, with resistless
navies, and with all the wealth and means that the highest civilization
of the world has accumulated. The ability, if they had the desire, of
either France or England or Germany to overwhelm the comparatively
weak nationalities of Central or South America can not be doubted.

It is a matter of profound concern to our country what should be
our attitude to the questions and controversies that arise between these
powerful European governments, on the one hand, and the weaker
nationalities of the American continent on the other.

The recent unpleasantness over the Venezuelan boundary, happily,
by the good sense and sober second thought of the English and American people, now in the process of a peaceful solution, has brought the
attention of the entire community to the consideration of the principles

that underlie this whole subject, and that are of the highest importance to the welfare of this country and the peace of the world.

When Mr. Olney asserts in his letter to Lord Salisbury that "to-day the United States is practically sovereign on this continent, and its fiat is law upon the subjects to which it confines its interposition;" and when the president practically asserts that the Monroe doctrine has become a part of international law; if these assertions are true, the position of the United States is certainly one of great responsibility, and of very doubtful advantage to compensate for the obligations that it incurs.

I believe the more correct statement of the fact is that the Monroe doctrine is a political dogma, and that like all dogma, it is subject to growth and development. Its interpretation is always very largely determined by the conditions at the time, and the circumstances attending any case to which it is sought to be applied. That the United States should look with disfavor upon every attempt of an European nation to oppress or despoil without right any American state, is inevitable. When such a controversy is pushed to its utmost limit, the unselfish defense of the weak against the strong, even to the extremity of war, is alike a wise and honorable policy for us as a nation, and it will surely command the support of the American people. But there should be no mistake about the principle upon which this policy rests. It is not at all that "the United States is sovereign on this continent," and it is not at all that we have the right or the duty to control the negotiations or treaties that other sovereign states may see fit to enter into. It is the just interest that we, as the foremost nation in America, have a right to take, and wisely take, in the free and unrestrained development of the institutions and commerce and prosperity of every American people. In the long future such a development is sure to be, in many ways, of the highest importance to us as a nation.

The assertion of this national policy in the past has been in every instance opportune, and in its results has commanded recognition of its wisdom. It matters not by what name we call the doctrine—its substance is that we have a direct concern in preserving the integrity and free development of every American nationality, and that as occasion arises we will interpose for the accomplishment of that object.

The distinguished citizen whom we are here to honor has been known among those who would be ready, perhaps eager, to assert the right of our country to intervene in questions of this character. We may properly express to him the hope and belief that he will in the discharge of his high duties, firmly, but temperately, stand for the American principle which finds its common expression in the saying, "America for the Americans."

MAYOR CALDWELL:

The next toast is "The Law-making Power" of our country. Who so capable of responding to this toast as our beloved fellow-citizen, the ideal lawyer, the Hon. John W. Warrington! (Cheers and applause.)

Speech by Hon. J. W. Warrington.

THE LAW-MAKING POWER, HON. JOHN W. WARRINGTON.

" Law is the supreme will of the people, expressed
through their legislative bodies."

We have no public power whose existence is so necessary and
whose exercise is watched with so much anxiety as that wielded by our
legislative bodies. Is this owing wholly to perverseness of political
parties, to selfish influences, to want of patriotism, or to all combined?
Is it not due in large part to the indifferent way in which we regard
and study the power? Shall we ever, as a nation, consider special
training as always requisite to the science of legislation, as we do with
respect to every other science or art, as also every occupation? We
select some great legislators. But have they predominated? Lord
Campbell, when sitting as chief justice of the Queen's Bench, said of
certain acts of Parliament : " One-half of our time is consumed in
making sense of other people's nonsense." This is largely true in our
own country. An instance occurred in England, where a penalty was
claimed under a statute which declared that of any penalty recovered
under it one-half was to go to the Crown and one-half to the informer.
What was the feeling of both the informer and the Crown when they
learned that the only penalty mentioned in the act was two years'
imprisonment ?

The right to make laws is the greatest of sovereign powers. No
matter through what agency legislative power has ever been exercised,
it has always controlled, and it must always control, the vital relations
and the destiny of mankind. The trend of modern civilization, not to
mention ancient instances, has been more and more toward confining
the power within the limits of constitutions. These constitutions are in
theory founded upon the consent of the governed. In order to ascertain
the true limit of the law-making power under any constitution it is

necessary to know not only its exact scope as an entirety, but also where the right to amend it resides. For illustration, in England, Germany and France this right to amend is given to the legislative bodies themselves. True, in Germany and France certain peculiarities as to form and majority must be observed, and in Germany it is claimed by some commentators that the Emperor may defeat a change by refusing to promulgate the act. But it is plain that the legislator there may regard the ultimate limits of his constitution with more or less indifference, for, after all, an infraction would be but a potential change.

In view of the conditions prevailing here, it is difficult for us fully to understand the nature of legislative power which includes the making of both organic and ordinary law. We have set bounds for our legislatures, and, indeed, for ourselves. We have done this through written constitutions defining powers, and through declarations respecting certain inalienable rights, for the government both of the United States and of the states themselves. The power to change these instruments is guarded by modes fixed for referring proposed amendments, either directly or indirectly, to the people themselves. Thus constitutional law can not be made in this country by any legislative body alone.

This limitation of the power of amendment in our country marks another important distinction between the law-making power here and that in the other countries named. If a legislative body here usurp a power not granted or violate an inhibition made by the constitution governing it, the judiciary is bound, whenever a proper case comes before it, to declare the statute void. And we have a universal custom thereupon to treat the statute as abolished. Our respected citizen, Mr. Bowler, has the courage to insist upon the right of an officer to determine the validity of a statute which he is called on to carry out. If it is not within constitutional limits it is not a law. If, therefore, he is not right, at least to the extent of referring the act to the judiciary, then what becomes of the boasted safeguards of a written constitution? But where the power to amend the constitution resides in a legislative body, that body itself becomes the final interpreter of its own action, and consequently the supreme power.

It is therefore even more important that the legislator in our Congress should be able to interpret and elucidate the constitution of the United States, than it is for the legislator in any one of the other countries I have mentioned, to understand his constitution. It should be no less true of the American than it was of the Roman Senator, of whom Cicero said that: "It is necessary for a senator to be thoroughly acquainted with the constitution; and this is a knowledge of the most extensive nature; a matter of science, of diligence, of reflection, without which no senator can possibly be fit for his office."

In order to take an active and intelligent part in legislation in our Congress one must have unusual ability and training. It calls for more than the faculty of criticism. It demands creative intellectual power. This power is rare. This power involves the faculty of seeing a public need and of originating an accurate plan to supply it. According as such a need increases in importance, so the minds fit to cope with it become fewer.

Philosophers differ as to the true principle of reasoning in legislation. For instance, Herbert Spencer differed in this regard from Jeremy Bentham. But, remembering that Lord Macaulay placed the latter in "the same rank with Gallileo and with Locke," no one would question the correctness of Bentham, who said, in respect of legislation: "To know what is good for the community whose welfare is at stake constitutes the science; to find the means of producing that good constitutes the art." When we apply this test to the demands and welfare of seventy millions of people; when we understand that the legislator must know what is wise and effectual for that vast body and what effect his proposed statute will have upon all other existing statutes; when we reflect that his action must conform with certain delegated powers of a written constitution, according as that instrument is construed by the judiciary; when these things are all considered, then we shall gain some adequate idea of the character of duty which a competent legislator has to perform.

But we still have only partially considered his functions. The power we are examining is to be exercised in the upper branch of the American Congress. The Senate possesses also certain executive and judicial powers. These are not within my subject. I may say, however, that it was thought by Alexander Hamilton that they would overshadow the legislative power. But great as those two powers are the other has kept pace with and surpassed them in importance. All these powers combined were originally intended to be the conservative force, the anchorage between the lower house of Congress and the

Executive. But while this is true in theory, would it not be more so in practice if our Senators were elected directly by the people? Practically speaking, Ohio has just furnished an example. For who, during the last year, was in doubt as to the Senatorship?

Yet in spite of custom or courtesy, of petty jealousies or differences, of individual cases of demagogy or buffoonery, which temporarily shadow that body, the Senate as a "check and balance" in our system of popular government still stands unrivaled.

Naturally such a place would attract great men. It brings its members into touch with the leading questions of the day. It affords competent and conscientious men the opportunity to render valuable service to their country. It presents rare chances for cultivating political science, statesmanship and the highest type of forensic debate. When dominated by strong and patriotic men it opens a fruitful field for the highest aims of laudable ambition.

An Englishman's denial of any right in the Crown to govern except by law, was once illustrated to me by his saying: "I pass the Prince with indifference; I pass the Premier or Judge with lifted hat." Indeed, when rightly considered, what aim could be loftier than a desire to make wise laws for the United States? Ours is a Government of law. Our sovereign is the law. True, as Mr. Lincoln said this is a "Government of the people, by the people, for the people." Yet the people govern through law. They yield to no earthly power except the law. It is part of the high office, then, of a Senator properly to interpret the reason of the people, their common consciousness of right and policy. Resolving this into form is the expression of the American sovereign. It at once becomes the idol and master of a vast Nation.

No higher testimony can be given of the importance of such a scene of action than the names of great men who have been actors in the Senate. Webster and Clay, Sumner and Fessenden, Pinckney and Calhoun, Douglass and Benton, Conkling and Blaine, Chase and Pugh, Wade and Ewing, Matthews, Pendleton and Thurman are some who have gone, and John Sherman is one who remains, of our illustrious line of American Senators.

Ohio has just called to that body Joseph Benson Foraker. With a remarkable record as soldier, lawyer and judge, as governor and orator, possessing wide culture and striking versatility, he is splendidly equipped for leadership in the Senate of the United States. While he will not have to debate some of the great questions whose discussion made some of his predecessors immortal, and whose solution was wrought in the blood and treasure of the country, yet we still have questions of vast moment. Think of the example recently given of the ease with which the country, although nearly defenseless, could be launched into serious war. Think of what can be done by the law-making power toward providing for arbitrating international disputes, and toward procuring national defensive means when that plan fails. Think of the stimulus the law-making power can give to an American merchant marine, which could also be chartered with conditions for naval service in times of war. Think of the strengthening arm the law-making power can extend to the judiciary in repressing and controlling menacing social disorders. Think of the great questions of finance, especially of the importance of a measure to forever destroy the heresy that unequal things can be made equal by law. Think of the important economic questions which involve both our external and internal schemes of taxation. Think of a great Government like ours in piping times of peace borrowing money to pay current expenses. These and kindred problems call for the analysis of masterful and patriotic minds.

We predict that Senator Foraker will contribute largely to their true solution. There is abundant room for the full play of his marked intellectual supremacy and acknowledged patriotism. He was supported and chosen for this high position by an unprecedented following and vote. We wish him God-speed.

MAYOR CALDWELL:

The next toast, "Our Internal Commerce," will be responded to by one of our most distinguished, most enterprising and most successful citizens, the Hon. M. E. Ingalls. (Cheers and applause.)

M. E. INGALLS.

Speech by Hon. M. E. Ingalls.

OUR INTERNAL COMMERCE,   HON. M. E. INGALLS.

"Commerce and industry are the best of a nation."

MR. CHAIRMAN, MY FRIENDS AND FELLOW-CITIZENS :

I would suggest that those of you who are tired go home, and let the balance of us have a night of it. At this hour of night and in this condition of the atmosphere, it will be impossible to make one heard unless we have your closest attention, and I have a very carefully prepared speech which will last for a long time.

This entertainment is divided into two parts ; you have had a committee who have been very careful in preparing it ; they have labored hard, and one of the conditions was that all early speeches should be carefully written out and submitted to a committee and after that they put in poor Melish and myself and told us we might go as we please. (Applause.)

They have had one of the most beautiful models for speaking that ever was in the city ; I suppose every one of you read the *Commercial-Gazette*—if you do not, you ought to—and I do not charge anything for this advertisement. (Laughter.) A few days ago, they had an editorial, telling what an after-dinner speech ought to be. I understand that that was so important that it was submitted to the Directors of that company, and they were not quite sure of it and then they sent for General Ryan and asked him to look it over. (More laughter.) He is the Ward McAllister of Cincinnati on after-dinner speeches, and he said this course was right, and the result is that every speech this evening has been hewed on that line. Now, I am afraid that my friend, the Mayor, may think I am getting off the track and intend to talk about the city government and taxation. (Renewed laughter.) But you need not be afraid, I shall not say anything wrong. I am like the girl who started out in the early morning with her bloomers on, to take a spin on her bicycle. She met a minister—one of those people who can never see anything good in matters out of the usual course—and he said to her: "Miss, don't you think bloomers are wicked?" "Well," she said, "Parson, I don't know what you might have found in some, but there is nothing wicked in mine." (Long and continuous applause and laughter.)

So I can say to you, gentlemen, that you can listen with composure, there is nothing bad in my speech. I am very glad to be here, however and pay my tribute to our guest—not because he is a Republican Senator—for I did not vote for him—not because he is a distinguished Republican, for I am a Democrat, and he has said many unkind things of my party in his day, but he is no sneak and you always know where to find him. He has been a bold, manly fighter in politics and has given and taken. But I come here tonight with great pleasure to join in this celebration, because he is my friend and neighbor and I know him and love him for that. (Cheers and applause.) And I believe in dinners like this and believe that if you have a friend that you love, you should say so, and say so in the morning and before he gets too old to enjoy it. (Applause.) And in this city we have not had, perhaps, too many great men, and it is just as well that we should pay our tribute to those that we have and thereby we may teach others to go and do likewise. I hope for him in his career everything that he wishes.

The career of a statesman is like a traveler climbing a mountain that reaches into the snow-clad air. It is a long and weary way, and if by chance he slips in climbing, he goes down to an unknown grave, politically. In these days, when the reporter is everywhere, when the telegraph flashes all over the country every word that is said, it requires something more of capacity to be a statesman than it did in the days of Webster and Clay, when they delivered a speech and took a week to revise it, and then gave it to the newspapers. (Cheers and applause and laughter.) So I hope that our friend may reach the summit of that mountain that he is climbing, and when he gets to the top let the plaudits of the world satisfy him. That is not everything that we work for; in life there are many things that we strive for. Life is made up of various things, "honest love, honest work for the day, honest hopes for the morrow. Are these worth nothing more than the hand they make weary, the heart they have saddened, the life they leave dreary.' No, there is something else that man works for and the reward he works for, the reward that he prizes more than anything is the respect and good will of his friends and neighbors. (Cheers and applause.)

And our friend may go forth to Washington as your Senator—in later years he may reach a still higher place, and I hope, personally, he may. (Renewed cheers and applause.) But no matter what honors may come to him, no matter what crowns may hereafter reward him, he will turn back to this hour as the happiest of his life.

He has been tried by his neighbors and they have approved of him. No higher commendation can a man want than that. And when he goes down to that Senate in Washington, I hope he will carry with him the same vigor and the same keenness for fight he has always had. I know of no body on earth that needs a man of his intellect, of his intellectuality and brain more than the Senate of the United States. (Long and continuous cheers and applause.) It looks to me as though the moss of years, as though the fruit of egotism has gathered there, as though communism and populism were making their last stand in the Senate of the United States, and I am glad that we are sending out from Ohio and from the city of Cincinnati, a man who can lead and, if necessary, fulfill the essential requirements of present demands.

You have all read the story told by Macaulay of the old cavaliers of England, who were driven out of England by Cromwell's troops; they went to Germany and France and, while there, they saw these same soldiers drive before them the French and achieve victory. Although they were exiles and in a strange land, yet they were filled with delight that it was England that was winning the battle. So as our friend goes down to Washington to the Senate, while those who are Democrats may heave a sigh that he is not of our political faith, we will still rejoice that he is from Cincinnati. (Cheers and applause.)

But, gentlemen, I was told to speak upon the internal commerce of this country. (Laughter.) Why, on the twenty-second day of February shall we talk dollars and cents? What we need in Cincinnati is not trade, but more public spirit. (Applause.) What we need is not so many millionaires as a higher citizenship. (Renewed applause.) If I were going to pick out the best things in the history of our guest tonight, I should say that in his administration as Governor, the

Bi-partisan Police Bill was passed, and the Police Commissioners were appointed ; the Bi-partisan Board of Elections were appointed ; the Board of Public Works, that laid our streets and expended our four million dollars, were appointed by him, and he can put these three things in his crown and wear them, for they are the best he will have. (Cheers and applause.)

And now, gentlemen, I will not talk shop to you tonight. I might tell you that the great line from here to Washington is the Chesapeake and Ohio. (Laughter.) I might talk about the steel rails, the electric lighted trains, and trains on time. We will take the Governor down there, and if you all want to go and see him inaugurated, you can all go for a reasonable compensation. (More laughter.) But this is the night of all others, as I say, when our thoughts should turn to our country. One hundred and sixty-four years ago was born the greatest patriot that ever lived, and we should think of him and turn our thoughts to better things. "Let the men who are men who hate meanness and lying be true to the vision that Washington saw." It is well that once in a while we should turn our eyes from trade and traffic and turn them back to the history of our country and resolve that we will establish here a higher citizenship—that we will do more for humanity. What we ask here is, that our guest should lead and we will follow. (Cheers and applause.)

MAYOR CALDWELL:

The next speaker—Col. Wm. B. Melish will respond to the toast "The Croaker." Col. Melish needs no introduction to a Cincinnati audience. He has been successful in commercial life ; prominent in social affairs ; and we presage for him a very honorable and brilliant military career. Now that he is promoted to that exalted military position of Colonel—Gentlemen—I present Col. Wm. B. Melish.

W. E. MELISH

Speech by Col. W. B. Melish.

THE CROAKER, . Col. W. B. Melish.

> " An old frog lived in a dismal swamp
> In a dismal kind of a way ;
> And all he did, whatever befell
> Was to croak the live long day."

Mr. Chairman and Gentlemen :

I am aware that it lacks but a few minutes of Sunday, therefore, as soon as the noise made by the Sunday-School scholars leaving the hall permits, we will proceed with the next toast of the evening, " The Croaker."

I have approached this topic with a great deal of doubt and misgivings of mind, but, after hearing the distinguished speaker who preceded me speak on the subject of "Internal Commerce," much after the style of Petroleum V. Nasby's lecture on " Milk," which even a cow could not recognize, (laughter) I have come to the conclusion that all you have to do is to go ahead as you please, and never allude to your subject.

I have studied a good deal over the ways of the " Croaker." It is the toughest thing I ever tackled. I have talked about a great many things, but how or why a man should talk about the " Croaker " at a congratulatory banquet, is a conundrum to me.

In time of distress you call on your friends, so I called first on the Mayor, the chairman of the committee, who addressed me as "*Colonel*," in capital letters, and then asked me to respond to this toast. I said : " Mr. Mayor, what are your ideas about croakers ; you are trying to run this town and consequently see lots of them ; therefore, what is a croaker ?" He said : " Look in the dictionary." We were standing in front of the Gibson House, and I said : " I have been to the dictionary, that is the slang dictionary, and it says : 'To croak is to die with a gurgling, rattling sound in your throat,'" (laughter), and, although standing in the presence of a Colonel, the Mayor suggested nothing which would make either a gurgle or a rattle, although I was ready to furnish the throat. (Renewed laughter). The Mayor said that the gentlemen responsible for this thing was General Hickenlooper ; that he, the General, was rather stuck on getting up toasts to which he could not respond himself, and that he fired them at his unsuspecting friends. So I went down to see the General, and he said : "That is one of the greatest toasts you ever heard of." I said : "Well, what is your idea about a croaker ?" And he said : "It is enough for my great intellect to get up the toast, and not to furnish the speech." (More laughter).

> "An old frog lived in a dismal swamp,
>   In a dismal kind of a way ;
> And all he did, whatever befell,
>   Was to croak the live-long day."

Who would have supposed that the President of the Gas Company would ever waste the gray matter of his brain on a toast like that? Can anybody imagine that a man, who is at the head of a corporation which pays twelve per cent. dividends is a croaker, and croaks *all* the time? We can readily imagine that if it was a "dismal *swamp*" that it was the wrecking of some opposition company. I said, "General, if you *are* responsible for this, give me an idea ;" and, says he, "I will tell you a croaker story : A fellow met a friend who was a chronic kicker, and he said to him, 'I had a dream about you last night.' 'Well, what did you dream?' 'I dreamt that I was in Heaven,' and the other said, 'Well, that was pretty good for you, what else?' 'Yes,' said the fellow, 'and the most singular thing was that you were in Heaven too.' 'Do tell,' says the other fellow, 'and what was I doing?' 'Oh, doing just like you were always doing here on earth — grumbling. There you were, sitting by the throne, and I distinctly heard you say, 'Why in the devil don't they make these halos so they will fit?'" (Laughter). Now, that was the General's idea of a croaker. Then I thought I would go to our mutual friend, the Honorable Jimmy Glenn, but the Honorable James said that since his hard job of enlightening the dear public about the Price Hill tanks, his own "think-tank" was out of order ; that he had not had an idea since then, and he declined "wid tanks." Thinking that a croaker who was living in a dismal swamp would like to get out, either by an aqueduct or a viaduct, I thought I would go and see a man who is an authority in the viaduct business, and so I hunted him up. I understood that he was something of a croaker, and, to be perfectly " Frank," I had to "Alter" all that. Then I was directed down on Third street, to another good " Citizen," for authority on Water Works, and there I found that the Circuit Court had "Ampt"-u-tated that authority. Dr. Graydon, who is always solicitous about budding orators, offered to loan me a poem on " Pessimism," but I declined solely in your interest, gentlemen, because I have always held the Doctor as an authority on poetry, especially since his two o'clock a. m. effort at the " Burns Club," where he asserted that the " Immortal Bobby " was the authority of the lines,

> "A mon 's a mon, for a' that and a' that,
> Be he a Republican or a Democrat."

I have come to the conclusion that there are no croakers here in Cincinnati. I am certainly not one, and, if I was, I could never croak on an occasion like this. I doubt if we can find a man or woman, Democrat or Republican, black or white, who has any croak coming at all because J. B. Foraker has been elected Senator. Why in the mischief they should put down a toast like this on an occasion like this, is more than I can understand. I have come to the conclusion that the only thing to do is to follow M. E. Ingall's "vestibuled-throughout, Chesapeake and Ohio " style, and get off the track, run on a switch and abandon the subject entirely. (Long and continuous cheers, applause and laughter). I conclude that the best thing to do is to talk about the Day, George Washington's, and I propose to organize a new society — Americans are great on societies — and I shall call it " The Sons of Evolution." I have already decorated the Governor of Ohio and the Mayor, and the Senator-elect wears the badge of the society. Look upon these hatchets, these cherries, and these twigs, and with bowed heads think of what they mean. This is *our* day ; we are the lineal descendants of the truth tellers of George Washington's time. The reason we are called " Sons of Evolution " is because history says that George Washington could not tell a lie — when he was a boy — but after he had grown up, had gone into politics, and got an office — well, history is silent, and wisely so. (Laughter and applause). I wanted the Governor especially to wear this badge, because during his term of office he will not have to tell a lie — that is if he will rely on his four generals and his eighteen colonels. I am sure that even if you cannot all be "Sons of Evolution" you will join us in an Ode to the natal day of our mutual friend.

TO WASHINGTON.

"Washington, yours was a noble deed.
Your cherry tree and ax have sown the seed
Of rectitude within the youthful mind,
Which might have been to other thoughts inclined.
But George, dear boy, for each one you've inspired,
Pray, don't forget, you've made the balance of us tired."

MORAL.

The moral is, that you need never tell a lie when the old man has cherry trees to burn. (Cheers and applause).

As none of you are leaving the room, as I had expected, permit me to again allude to "Croakers." Going back to the dictionary about the "Croakers," I learned in my wanderings around Old Point Comfort, (and this is no advertisement of the Chesapeake and Ohio Road), that the "Croaker" is a fish, which is frequently caught down there, which Colonel Billy Walker says "tastes something between a seahorse and a boiled rubber over-shoe," and which, by authority of Mr. Ingalls, is served upon the Pullman dining-cars on that road, but, as I said, to return, not to our fish, but our croaker. In any and all the relations of life, the croaker has a prominent place — more's the pity. Your average croaker is merely a pessimist gone to seed. Graduating as a pessimist, he fills his pockets with bombs and becomes an Anarchist. When he becomes bilious and feels mean, he is satisfied that he is either too good or pious for the balance of us ; or else he feels patriotism, of the croaker stamp : is concerned about the good of his party, and wants an office, so that he can reform it.

He feels like he is a new man in opposition to the new woman, and,

" While his wife takes in sewing, to keep things agoing, the croaker superintends the earth." He is like a mustard plaster, in that he has no curative properties, but is simply a counter-irritant, and also, like a mustard plaster, he is usually raising hell behind your back. (Laughter and applause).

In a battle — I do not speak now in my military capacity, but rather of business or political battles -- while others carry arms, the croaker shoulders a telescope that he may foresee disaster, looks wise and prophesies defeat, and lets out section after section, that he may magnify awful disaster out of the minor weaknesses of his brethren. He, too, would be a soldier, were it not for the fact that his grandfather met with an accident, and he has inherited the symptoms. (Laughter).

As a politician he understands the villainies of all other parties, and is utterly ignorant of the good things of his own. He is as badly off in his definitions of things as the little girl in the Parish Church, who had carefully been drilled to answer correctly the one question in the Catechism which the teacher supposed would be propounded to her, but, unfortunately, the little girl ahead of her was absent, and so, instead of being asked by the Priest, " What is Purgatory?" she caught the question " What is Matrimony?" and she responded. " That state of torment in which souls are punished for their sins." " Tut, tut," said the father, " that is the answer to Purgatory." But the Bishop, who was doubtless more experienced, said, " Howld on, let the child alone, for all you and I know, she is telling the truth." ' Laughter and applause).

But, brethren, it is your business croaker who is the typical cuss alluded to in the sentiment accompanying this toast, who sits in the swamp *all* the day long and does nothing but croak. He pervades commercial and financial centers and with his depressing outlook, flaps the owl wings of gloom in the face of a rising sun of Prosperity, and declares that financial disaster is the unquestioned interpretation of Daniel's dream, and that the weird beast with seven heads and ten horns is to trample the credit of business circles in the dust. Your croaker is a hybrid sort of an animal, like a bat, half mouse and half bird ; he is not a first-class flyer, and as a sprinter he is a dismal failure.

And yet this good old government can borrow a hundred million of dollars any day from we bloated aristocrats, and we still have money for banquets.

The croaker is always ready to add to disaster, whether justified or not. He is as bad as the man whose wife sent him down to the cellar for a pitcher of milk. He stumbled unfortunately on the top step, and he went down into the cellar, with such casual interruption to his career as each step afforded as he struck them in succession. As he lit on the stone pavement of the bottom, he was comforted by his wife asking him, with that tender solicitude which wives can assume on like occasions : "John, did you break the pitcher?" and John said, "Naw, I didn't, but d——d if I don't ;" and he did. (Laughter and applause).

Whatever hindrances there are in our municipal affairs, our business advance and our commercial interests as a city, they have been and are largely due to the croakers who lay down when the columns of united interests are ordered to advance. Let us hope that all the sore spots which the croaker exhibits will be made by the heels of enterprise, which trample him into the dust on their onward march to success. (Applause). The average croaker is an ambulance with a loud gong, going about the streets but belonging to no hospital. But let us dismiss the croaker, and bury him under the ruins of any business which he murders. On his tombstone let an inverted hand be carved, its fingers pointing downward, and over it the legend : "Buried with the burial of an ass ;" and under it his last words : "I told you so."

My brethren, fluctuations in demand may in time deceive even an optimist as to the possible supply. Over production must necessarily depreciate values, adverse conditions and very strained relations may sometimes be very hard to bring into close fellowship, yet, while the day may be protracted between seed time and harvest, between invest-ment and return, the return comes when energy is wedded to an unfal-tering determination to win, and Mahomet will start for the mountain, when he has ascertained that the mountain has no intention of moving toward him.

Now a few words in conclusion. I don't know whether the Senator-elect would like to have any advice about his course in the Senate from the croakers present, but we are ready to give it to him if he wants it. We would like to suggest, when he goes to Washington, that he arrange to have a government under which we can have an American chance to earn a living, and the right to keep it when we earn it. We would get it honestly, of course. We would also like his help to make this country the best place on earth to live in, to work in, and to die in; and the other little places, which we have not annexed, like Venezuela and Cuba, can wait a short time, until we have straightened these things out.

As to our brother Foraker, he has heard a few only of the good things of himself in which we all concur. We do not begrudge him these because we all love him, and, like my distinguished friend, Sir Henry Irving, as quoted to me by his friend, Dr. Graydon :

> "Give me my sword, ' Excalibur,"
> Why listen to this ' Cro-aker,'
> Are we not all tried, trusty friends,
> A toast to him, our ' For-aker.' "   (Laughter).

Brother Foraker has been sentenced by the people to a term of six years in the Senate, for his repeatedly expressed contempt of the High Court of the Democracy. He says he doesn't know just what he will do there or how he will do it. It strikes the average Republican that if any one crosses swords with the Senator-elect, it will be a case of what the *other* fellow will do. We commend such to a study of the doughty warrior in " Twelfth Night," for he will doubtless have occasion to say, " Plague on 't, and I thought he had been valiant and so cunning in fence, I 'd have seen him hanged ere I 'd have challenged him."

If Brother Foraker has any trouble about the distribution of the offices, either local or otherwise, we can assure him he need not worry about that. If he will select any three or four of the gentlemen present to-night, we will gladly attend to all such matters for him, and thus save him a great deal of trouble and correspondence.

But let us call a truce to all this pleasantry and jest. We are to end this delightful opportunity of laying our garlands of love and respect at the feet of our neighbor, our friend, our brother — brother in the great fellowship of the universal brotherhood of man ; banded to make each other happier and the world better by our living in it. We have given our honored guest our sincere congratulations. We send to that noble woman who has been, and is, the inspiration of his public and private life, our heart echoed wishes that all happiness, health and prosperity may be the measure given the home circle for many, many years.

In this, the closing hour of night, our closing words to brother Foraker are, that either here, or in Washington, or wherever he is ;

> " Our hearts, our hopes are all with thee,
> Our hearts, our hopes, our prayers, our tears,
> Our faith triumphant o'er our fears,
> Are all with thee, are all with thee."

(Cheers and applause).

List of Guests.

Ayres, James M.
Ampt, Wm. M.
Alter, Franklin.
Allison, Robert.
Altenberg, Geo. P.
Archibald, R. M.
Alms, Fred. H.
Ackerland, Max.
Alms, Wm. H.
Addy, Matthew.
Archibald, R. J. H.
Butterfield, A. P.
Brown, Dan'l W.
Bradford, E. F.
Bullock, George.
Bettinger, Albert.
Bernard, Lewis G.
Breen, John.
Braemer, Theo.
Buckland, Geo.
Burch, Wallace.
Bushnell, A. S.
Burton, Stephen R.
Bode, A. H.
Buchwalter, M. L.
Burgheim, Max.
Bailey, Sam'l, Jr.

Bauer, Morris
Bosworth, C. A.
Brown, Chas. Edgar.
Bundy, Wm. E.
Bromwell, J. H.
Bradley, F. A.
Brannan, J. D.
Ballman, F. H.
Bettman, Morris L.
Brown, Adolph L.
Biddle, W. P.
Bettman, B.
Black, L. C.
Brewster, J. W.
Bader, Fred.
Bohrer, Geo. H.
Carl, Alvin.
Colter, Archibald.
Cox, Benj. H.
Carroll, R.
Campbell, B. W.
Cox, Geo. B.
Cox, Joseph.
Carew, Jos. T.
Corre, A. G.
Colston, Edward.
Crane, Clinton.

Cox, Joseph, Jr.

Conroy, A. J.

Caldwell, John A.

Cushing, Wade.

Clore, J. C.

Comstock, F. D.

Crawford, L. J.

Commercial Gazette.

Critchell, B. P.

Davis, David.

Davis, Nat. Henchman.

Dana, S. F.

Du Brul, Nap'n.

Davidson, A.

Davis, Charles.

Dunbar, H. B.

Diem, F. J.

Dodds, Milo G.

Ermston, Jas. D.

Espy, James.

Ezekiel, H. C.

Ellison, Jas. D.

Emerson, Lowe,

Egan, Thos. P.

Ernst, Rich'd P.

Ehrman, Benj. F.

Ellis, Frank.

Ebersole, Geo. R.

Evans, Chas.

Ernst, John P.

Enquirer, The Cin'ti.

Freie Presse, The.

Foraker, J. B.

Freiberg, Maurice J.

Fisher, Wm. Hubbell.

Freiberg, J. W.

Felton, Sam'l M.

French, Tilden R.

Furst, Abe.

Ferris, Howard.

Fechheimer, J. S.

Fleischmann, Chas.

Fleischmann, Julius.

Fechheimer, Henry S.

Foraker, Jos. B., Jr.

Fisher, George.

Fitzgerald, J. W.

Frey, John.

Foraker, Jas. R.

Ford, Collin.

Ford, Wm.

Fries, Gus. R.

Fagin, Morgan H.

Fisk, Chas. H.

Garrard, Jeptha,

Griffith, G. P.

Guthrie, J. V.

Gano, Gazzam.

Goodman, Wm. A.

Goetz, John, Jr.

Graydon, Dr. T. W.
Gansel, Chas. O.
Gregg, E. B.
Grant, W. C.
Goldsmith, A. W.
Galvin, John.
Granger, W. W.
Gray, Adam.
Greenwald, C. E.
Gordon, W. J. M.
Goodale, Levi C.
Hoefinghoff, Chas.
Hooker, Jas. J.
Hunt, W. L.
Hoyt, Jas. H.,
Hall, E. C.
Hicks, James.
Harper, J. C.
Heuer, W. H.
Hunt, Chas. J.
Hadden, C. B.
Herrmann, Aug.
Hickenlooper, A.
Hinkle, A. Howard.
Hoffheimer, Harry M.
Hafer, George.
Holloway, C. M.
Herlinger, A. L.
Harrison, W. H.
Hendley, Frank W.

Hutton, J. M.
Hollister, Howard C.
Henshaw, George.
Huschart, Frank M.
Holmes, C. R.
Hutton, Wm. E.
Heekin, James.
Hunt, Samuel F.
Heath, Perry S.
Hertenstein, Fred.
Heath, Thos. F.
Harrison, Jos. T.
Ingalls, M. E.
Immenhart, Henry.
Isaacson, W. J.
Irwin, Wm. T.
Jones, Rankin D.
Jelke, Fred'k, Jr.
Johnson, J. W.
Jackson, W. H.
Knopf, Sam'l.
Kramer, Adam A.
Kuhn, Louis.
Kineon, Sol. P.
Kittredge, E. W.
Kenan, N. G.
Kellogg, Chas. H.
Keck, Lee R.
Kirchner, Frank.
Kilgour, John.

Kingsbury, C. G.
Kelley, Thos. H.
Kahn, Chas., Jr.
Kroger, B. H.
Kirchner, F. H.
Kurtz, Chas. L.
Krohn, M.
Kuhn, Oscar W.
Knaul, M.
Kunder, Judge Phil. H.
Kinsley, J. R.
Langdon, Perin.
Lewis, Eugene L.
Lippencott, W. J.
Laws, Harry L.
Lawson, F. H.
Lowenstein, Gus., Sr.
Lotze, C. M.
Luebbing. G. G.
Laidley, F. A.
Levy, James.
Logan, Thos. A.
Mayer, L.
Maxwell, S. N.
McCrea, C. T.
Mack, Thos. A.
Morrison & Co., James.
Melish, W. B.
McNeill, Aaron.
Mosby, John B.

Mullane, A. J.
Monfort, E. R.
Morgan, R. J.
Markbreit, Leopold.
Mulvihill, T. J.
McIntyre, Marion.
Mackey, John.
Mack, M. J.
Miller, I. J.
Mullen, Mike.
Murphy, John P.
Minor, Thos. C.
Martin, D. B.
McCally, E. L.,
McCormick, E. O.
Marfield, Elliott.
McDowell, Jos. J.
Nippert, C. L.
Oskamp, Henry.
Outcalt, Miller.
Prendergast, J. W.
Pfiester, Fred.
Peaslee, John B.
Pluemer, Adolph.
Prior, C. E.
Pugh, A. H.
Peters, Ralph.
Peabody, W. W.
Pistor, Wm.
Peebles, Jos. S.

Pullen, R. T.
Peck, Hiram D.
Paxton, Thos. B.
Pattison, John M.
Pedretti, R. M.
Post, The Cin'ti.
Ryan, Michael.
Ravolgi, A.
Rheinstrom, Sig.
Rettig, John.
Roth, E. N.
Roe, G. M.
Rosenbaum, Harry.
Rulison, H. M.
Rowe, Casper.
Robertson, C. D.
Rowe, W. S.
Ricketts, Merrill.
Robinson, J. M.
Rendigs, Wm.
Reamy, Dr. Thad. A.
Shattuck, W. B.
Shipherd, John J.
Strauss, Isa.
Swing, Jas. B.
Smith, Jackson.
Senior, Edw.
Schwill, Albert.
Swing, P. F.
Strunk, Wm.

Santmeyer, C. A
Sterritt, Geo. T.
Smith, Amor. Jr.
Scarlett, J. A.
Schmidlapp, J. G.
Stanley, H. J.
Smith, Rufus B.
Smith, J. H. Chas.
Stone, Geo. N.
· Sayler, John R.
Seasongood, Lewis.
Sullivan, John J.,
Smith, J. M.
Spiegel, Fred. S.
Stephens, Chas. H.
Sullivan, J. J.,
Shears, D. C.
Thrasher, A. B.
Trost, Sam'l W.
Taylor, J. Gordon.
Tullidge, Frank G.
Tucker, Alf. A.
Trost, Jacob.
Taft, Chas. P.
Tharp, Willis P.
Tribune, The Cin'ti.
Times-Star, The.
Traub, L.
Voorheis, A. B.
Vandergrift, Geo. A.

Volksblatt, The.
Volksfreund, The.
Weir, Fred. C.
Wright, D. Thew.
Wiborg, F. B.
Warrington, J. W.
Woodmansee, D. D.
Wilson, M. F.
Washburn, John B.
Webb, T. D.
Wulsin, Drausin.
Woods, Wm.
Whetstone, John C.

Winkler, Philip.
West, Robt. H.
Waddell, Robt. S.
White, Alfred.
Wilson, Robt.
Wabnitz, Geo.
Wilder, Stephen H.
Walker, Wm. P.
Vergason, H. C.
Zumstein, John.
Zumstein, Frank C.
Ziegler, H. M.

www.ingramcontent.com/pod-product-compliance
Lightning Source LLC
Chambersburg PA
CBHW020235090426
42735CB00010B/1704